DuckDB database: Learning SQL in CLI Client

Djoni Darmawikarta

Table of Contents

Introduction

Welcome to **DuckDB Database: Learning SQL in CLI Client**!

DuckDB is a relational database. It is an embedded database, there's no server software to install.

For example, when you run the following commands, a file, **bookdb**, will be created.

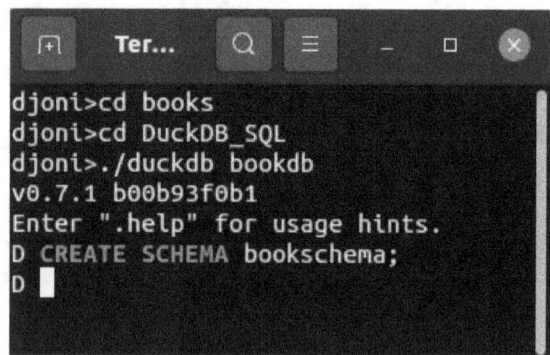

Here are the files in the DuckDB_SQL (sub)folder.

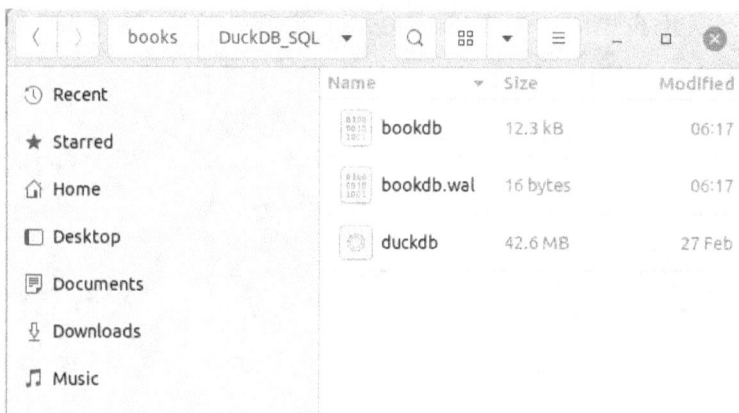

This single file is the DuckDB database, which will contain your tables, their data and other objects required by the database to function.

duckdb file is the DuckDB's CLI client (Command Line Interface) that you need to download from the DuckDB website. Read the Appendix at the last part of the book to get yourself initiated to the CLI.

The other file bookdb.wal is a temporary file, which will automatically be deleted when you finish using the bookdb database.

In this book I use CLI, but the SQL commands work the same on the other clients supported by DuckDB, such as C, Java, and R.

The Appendix is your guide to download and install the CLI. The download is one file named **duckdb**. This one downloaded file, the CLI, is all you need to start creating and using DuckDB database.

Chapter 1: Storing data

In a relational database like DuckDB, data is stored as table. A table has columns and rows. In this chapter you will learn how to create table using SQL, and then, to add data, update and delete them.

Database

Start your CLI client as follows. Mine is as follows. (I used Ubuntu and downloaded the CLI into books/DuckDB_SQL sub-folder)

Go to the (sub)folder where you have the downloaded CLI file. The ./duckdb bookdb command create a database named **bookdb.**

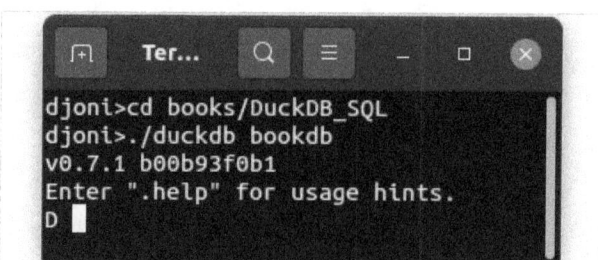

Schema

A database can have multiple schema. We want to keep all our database objects, such as tables and views, under **bookschema**. To create a schema, we use the SQL CREATE SCHEMA statement. As we want to use this schema for all examples, we set it as the default schema. Enter and execute the following two SQL commands.

```
djoni>cd books/DuckDB_SQL
djoni>./duckdb bookdb
v0.7.1 b00b93f0b1
Enter ".help" for usage hints.
D CREATE SCHEMA bookschema;
D SET SCHEMA TO bookschema;
D
```

Table

Now that we have a database and a schema under the database, we are ready to create a table under the schema. Name the table **product**. We use the SQL CREATE TABLE statement.

```
djoni>cd books/DuckDB_SQL
djoni>./duckdb bookdb
v0.7.1 b00b93f0b1
Enter ".help" for usage hints.
D CREATE SCHEMA bookschema;
D SET SCHEMA TO bookschema;
D CREATE TABLE product(
> p_code INTEGER,
> p_name VARCHAR,
> p_price DECIMAL,
> p_date DATE);
D
```

The product table will have four columns: p_code (stands for product code), p_name (product name), p_price, and launch_dt (the date the product was launched to the market), with their data types INT (integer), VARCHAR (variable length string), DECIMAL, and DATE, respectively. Note that these are four of the most commonly used data types; DuckDB supports some other data types.

Add data

Your product table is still empty. Let's insert (add) seven rows using the following SQL INSERT statement.

```
djoni>cd books/DuckDB_SQL
djoni>./duckdb bookdb
v0.7.1 b00b93f0b1
Enter ".help" for usage hints.
D CREATE SCHEMA bookschema;
D SET SCHEMA TO bookschema;
D CREATE TABLE product(
> p_code INTEGER,
> p_name VARCHAR,
> p_price DECIMAL,
> p_date DATE);
D INSERT INTO product VALUES
> (1, 'Nail', 10.0, '2013-03-31'),
> (2, 'Washer', 15.00, '2013-03-29'),
> (3, 'Nut', 15.00, '2013-03-29'),
> (4, 'Screw', 25.00, '2013-03-30'),
> (5, 'Super_Nut', 30.00, '2013-03-30'),
> (6, 'New Nut', NULL, NULL),
> (7, 'Other_Products', NULL, NULL);
D
```

To save some spaces in book pages and for better visualization, from now on I will not show the whole screenshot, I will only show the command being discussed and, if any, its response.

Query data

Let's check that the seven rows are inserted correctly by querying the table using the SQL SELECT statement.

```
D SELECT * FROM product;
```

p_code int32	p_name varchar	p_price decimal(18,3)	p_date date
1	Nail	10.000	2013-03-31
2	Washer	15.000	2013-03-29
3	Nut	15.000	2013-03-29
4	Screw	25.000	2013-03-30
5	Super_Nut	30.000	2013-03-30
6	New Nut		
7	Other_Products		

The response (or output, result, or more technically, the returned rows) is displayed on the console.

From now on, in this book, I will use "returned rows".

Update data

Next, as an exercise for you, let's update the price of p_code (product code) 7. You will change its name from 'Other_Products' to 'Others'.

If after executing the update, you query the product table, the name of that product should show 'Others'.

```
D UPDATE product SET p_name = 'Others' WHERE p_code = 7;
D SELECT * FROM product;
```

p_code int32	p_name varchar	p_price decimal(18,3)	p_date date
1	Nail	10.000	2013-03-31
2	Washer	15.000	2013-03-29
3	Nut	15.000	2013-03-29
4	Screw	25.000	2013-03-30
5	Super_Nut	30.000	2013-03-30
6	New Nut		
7	Others		

13

Delete data

Finally, before you learn and practice queries (the primary purpose of this book) in the upcoming chapters, let's delete this 'Others' product, the p_code of which is 7.

After executing the above command, if you query the product table, the 'Others' should no longer be there.

```
DELETE FROM product WHERE p_code = 7;
SELECT * FROM product;
```

p_code int32	p_name varchar	p_price decimal(18,3)	p_date date
1	Nail	10.000	2013-03-31
2	Washer	15.000	2013-03-29
3	Nut	15.000	2013-03-29
4	Screw	25.000	2013-03-30
5	Super_Nut	30.000	2013-03-30
6	New Nut		

In the next chapters we will use the above data for you to learn SQL queries.

Chapter 2: Queries on one table

You query (read data) using a SELECT statement.

Here's the syntax of a SELECT statement. SELECT and FROM are mandatory, WHERE and ORDER BY are optional. You will learn all of them in this chapter.

```
SELECT selected_list
FROM table
WHERE conditions
ORDER BY columns
;
```

Querying specific columns

The selected_list in a SELECT statement can be just columns from the table. In Example 2.1 the select_list is the two columns, p_name and p_price.

Example 2.1: Querying p_name and p_price columns

```
SELECT p_name, p_price FROM product;
```

Here is the result of the query:

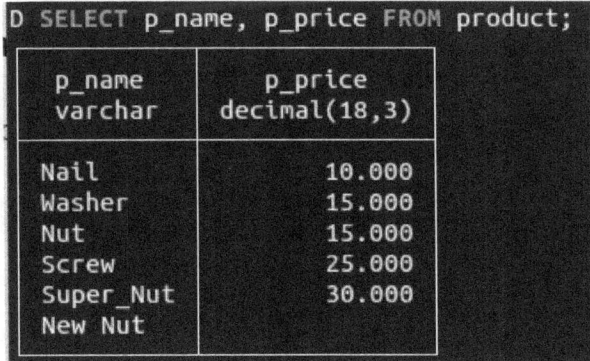

All columns

If you want to have all columns returned, then, instead of listing the columns, you can put * as the select list as demonstrated in Example 2.2.

Example 2.2: Querying all columns

```
SELECT * FROM product;
```

Here are the returned rows:

```
D SELECT * FROM product;

 p_code  | p_name    | p_price         | p_date
 int32   | varchar   | decimal(18,3)   | date

       1 | Nail      |         10.000  | 2013-03-31
       2 | Washer    |         15.000  | 2013-03-29
       3 | Nut       |         15.000  | 2013-03-29
       4 | Screw     |         25.000  | 2013-03-30
       5 | Super_Nut |         30.000  | 2013-03-30
       6 | New Nut   |                 |
```

Expressions

A select list does need to be just columns from the table, It can have an expression. An expression can for example be a calculation of net amount, i.e. price after tax, as in Example 2.3 below.

Example 2.3: Expression in select list

```
SELECT p_name, p_price + (p_price * 0.13) FROM product;
```

```
D SELECT p_name, p_price + (p_price * 0.13)  FROM product;

   p_name      (p_price + (p_price * 0.13))
   varchar              decimal(18,5)

   Nail                     11.30000
   Washer                   16.95000
   Nut                      16.95000
   Screw                    28.25000
   Super_Nut                33.90000
   New Nut
```

CASE expression

Expression on the select list can contain a logic using CASE.

CASE comes in two flavors: simple and search.

Simple CASE

Here is the syntax of a query with simple CASE.

```
SELECT columns,
  CASE column
    WHEN equal_value1
    THEN output_value1
    WHEN equal_value2
    THEN output_value2
    WHEN ...
    [ELSE else_value]
  END AS output_column
FROM table
WHERE ... ;
```

A SELECT query with a simple CASE produces a computed column with an *output_column* name as specified on the END AS.

The computation has the following logic:

The *column* in the CASE *column* is tested on its equality to the *equal_value* in the WHEN equal_value. If it equals to equal_value1 THEN the output_column is output_value1. If not, then it is tested against equal_value2. If equals then the output_column is output_value2, and so on. If not equal to the last output_value, then the output_column is else_value.

Please try Example 2.4 to practice your understanding about simple CASE.

Example 2.4: simple CASE

```
SELECT p_code, p_name,
CASE p_price WHEN 10 THEN 'Cheap'
  WHEN 15 THEN 'Medium'
  WHEN 25 THEN 'Expensive'
    ELSE 'Others'
  END AS price_cat FROM product;
```

The console below shows the returned row with the p_cat (price category) allocated to each of the products.

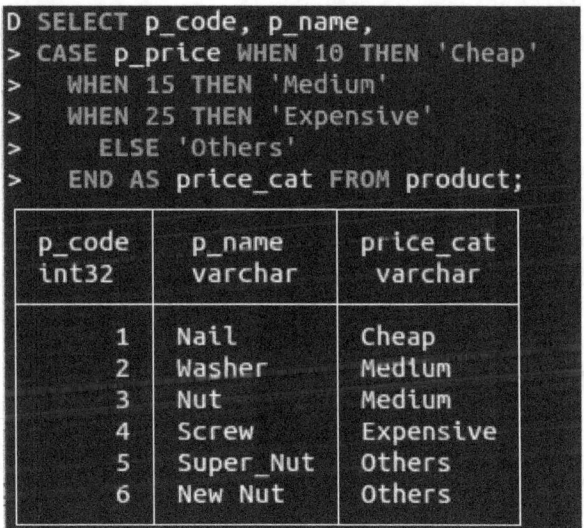

Searched CASE

Simple CASE compares the equality of a column (price column in the previous example) to one or more values. In searched CASE you can apply any condition. Here is the syntax for the Searched CASE.

```
SELECT columns,
  CASE
    WHEN condition1
    THEN output_value1
    WHEN condition2
    THEN output_value2
    WHEN ...
    ELSE else_value
  END AS output_column
FROM table
WHERE ... ;
```

The conditions are evaluated starting from the first WHEN and down to the last WHEN. If a WHEN condition is met, its THEN output_value is returned to the output_column and the CASE process stops. If none of the WHEN conditions is met, *else_value* is returned if there exists an ELSE clause. If no condition is met and no ELSE clause exists, NULL will be returned.

Example 2.5 below applies search CASE.

Example 2.5: search CASE

```
SELECT p_code,p_name,
CASE
 WHEN (p_price <= 10 AND p_name NOT LIKE 'Nut%')
   THEN 'Cheap'
 WHEN p_price BETWEEN 11 AND 25
   THEN 'Medium'  WHEN p_price > 25 THEN 'Expensive'
 WHEN p_price IS NULL AND p_date IS NULL
   THEN 'NA'
 ELSE 'Others'
   END AS price_cat
FROM product;
```

The returned rows are, as expected, correctly assigned their price category.

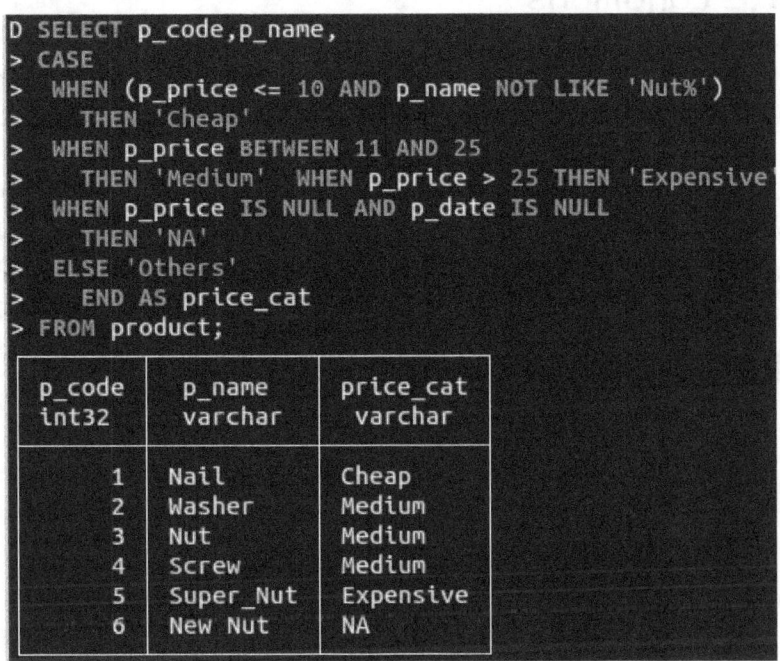

```
D SELECT p_code,p_name,
> CASE
>  WHEN (p_price <= 10 AND p_name NOT LIKE 'Nut%')
>    THEN 'Cheap'
>  WHEN p_price BETWEEN 11 AND 25
>    THEN 'Medium'  WHEN p_price > 25 THEN 'Expensive'
>  WHEN p_price IS NULL AND p_date IS NULL
>    THEN 'NA'
>  ELSE 'Others'
>    END AS price_cat
> FROM product;
```

p_code int32	p_name varchar	price_cat varchar
1	Nail	Cheap
2	Washer	Medium
3	Nut	Medium
4	Screw	Medium
5	Super_Nut	Expensive
6	New Nut	NA

WHERE conditions

While all previous example are about select_list, which are columns that you want on the returned rows, you use WHERE in a query to get only specific rows.

The examples so far returns all rows. If you need to query only certain rows, put a WHERE condition. In Example 2.6 below we query only products (query) with price less than 25.

Example 2.6: Querying rows with price < 25

```
SELECT p_name, p_price FROM product
WHERE p_price < 25
;
```

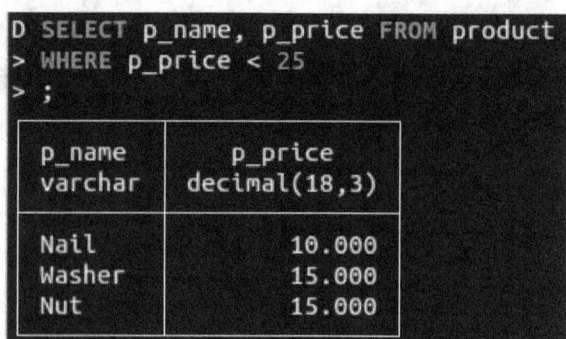

The condition in Example 2.6 above use < comparison operator. You can also use other comparison operators supported by DuckDB. Here the list of the comparison operators.

Operator	Description
=	Equal to
<	Less than
>	Greater than
<=	Less than or equal to
>=	Greater than or equal to
!=	Not equal to

Compound expressions

If you need to have more complex condition, use apply AND and OR logical operators to compound the conditions. Example 2.7 has AND and OR. As we want to find rows having launch date => '2013-03-30' or rows having price > 15, we compound these two conditions with OR. This compound condition is further AND compounded with the third condition (product name is not Nail). Hence, only rows that meets the two compounded conditions will be returned.

Example 2.7: Compound condition

```
SELECT * FROM product
WHERE
(p_date >= '2013-03-30'
OR p_price > 15)
AND (p_name != 'Nail')
;
```

You will get the two returned rows are as expected.

```
D SELECT * FROM product
> WHERE
> (p_date >= '2013-03-30'
> OR p_price > 15)
> AND (p_name != 'Nail')
> ;
```

p_code int32	p_name varchar	p_price decimal(18,3)	p_date date
4	Screw	25.000	2013-03-30
5	Super_Nut	30.000	2013-03-30

NOT logical operator

You can use NOT to negate a condition and return rows that do not satisfy the condition.

Example 2.8: NOT to negate the condition

```
SELECT * FROM product
WHERE
NOT
(p_date >= '2013-03-30'
OR p_price > 15)
AND (p_name != 'Nail')
;
```

Here are the returned rows.

```
D SELECT * FROM product
> WHERE
> NOT
> (p_date >= '2013-03-30'
> OR p_price > 15)
> AND (p_name != 'Nail')
> ;
```

p_code int32	p_name varchar	p_price decimal(18,3)	p_date date
2	Washer	15.000	2013-03-29
3	Nut	15.000	2013-03-29

BETWEEN Operator

The BETWEEN operator evaluates equality to any value within a range. The range is specified by a boundary, which specifies the lowest and the highest values.

Example 2.9: NOT to negate the condition

```
SELECT * FROM product
WHERE p_price BETWEEN 15 AND 25
;
```

You should see the correct returned rows the same as mine below.

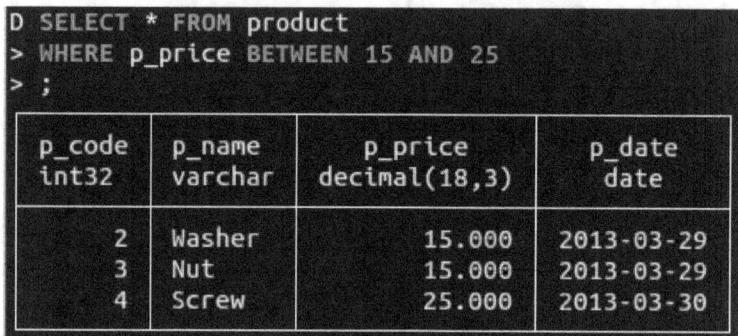

IN Operator

The IN operator compares a column with a list of values. In Example 2.10 you only want to grab rows that has these prices.

Example 2.10: IN operator

```
SELECT * FROM product
WHERE
p_price IN (10, 25, 50)
;
```

Only Nail and Screw that have prices 10 and 25 respectively meet the condition.

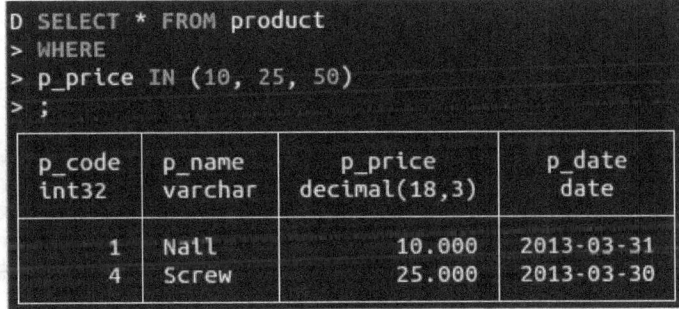

LIKE Operator

The LIKE operator allows you to specify an imprecise equality condition. The wildcard character can be a percentage sign (%) to represent any number of characters or an underscore (_) to represent a single occurrence of any character.

In Example 2.11 below, we want to query only products that have a name starting with N and contain only three characters, or starting with Sc and any number of characters after.

Example 2.11: LIKE wild characters

```
SELECT * FROM product
WHERE p_name LIKE 'N__'
OR p_name LIKE 'Sc%'
;
```

Nut qualifies the first LIKE condition, and Screw the second condition.

If you want to query names that have a wild character, such as the Super_nut that has an underscore, so that the _ is not mistaken as a wild character, use an ESCAPE **character,** this is the character as you define in the **ESCAPE** clause.

In Example 2.12 below we define $ as our escape character, hence in $_ the underscore is not a wild character, it is an underscore character.

Example 2.12: LIKE wild characters

```
SELECT * FROM product
WHERE
p_name LIKE '%$_%' ESCAPE '$'
;
```

Our query correctly caught the Super_Nut.

```
D SELECT * FROM product
> WHERE
> p_name LIKE '%$_%' ESCAPE '$'
> ;
```

p_code int32	p_name varchar	p_price decimal(18,3)	p_date date
5	Super_Nut	30.000	2013-03-30

NULL

NULL, an SQL reserved word, represents the absence of data. NULL is applicable to any data type. It is not the same as a numeric zero or an empty string or a 0000/00/00 date.

You can only test whether or not a column is NULL by using the IS NULL or IS NOT NULL operator. Example 2.13 has price IS NULL condition.

Example 2.13: price IS NULL

```
SELECT * FROM product
WHERE
p_price IS NULL
;
```

Only New Nut has NULL price, hence it is the only row returned by the query.

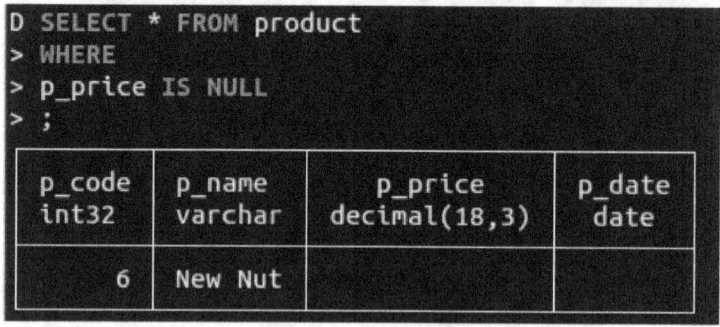

DISTINCT

A query might return duplicate rows, rows with columns containing exactly the same data. If you don't want to see duplicate output rows, use DISTINCT in your SELECT clause.

You can use DISTINCT on one column or multiple columns.

The query in Example 2.14 uses DISTINCT on the price column to find out the distinct prices from all rows. Turned out as the query found out that we have distinct prices.

Example 2.14: DISTINCT price

```
SELECT
DISTINCT p_price
FROM product
;
```

Our query correctly captures the four distinct prices.

DISTINCT on multiple columns

If you need to find out some distinct values based on a combination of columns, just use DISTINCT once at the beginning of the select list. Example 2.15 applies DISTINCT on two columns: price and launch_dt.

Example 2.15: DISTINCT on price and launch_dt combination

```
SELECT DISTINCT
p_price, p_date
FROM product
;
```

Our query found four distinct combinations.

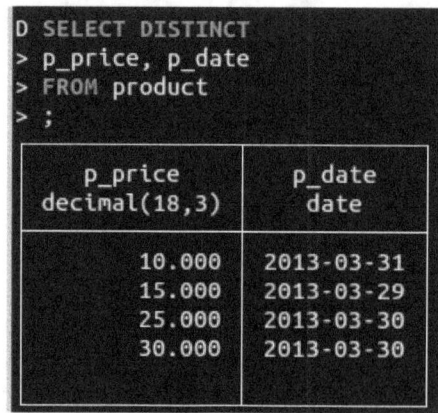

LIMIT

Use LIMIT to limit the number of returned rows.

In Example 2.16 below, instead of all rows, only first two rows are returned by the query thanks to the LIMIT 2.

Example 2.16: Limiting to 2 rows

```
SELECT * FROM product
LIMIT 2
;
```

Only two of the six rows are returned.

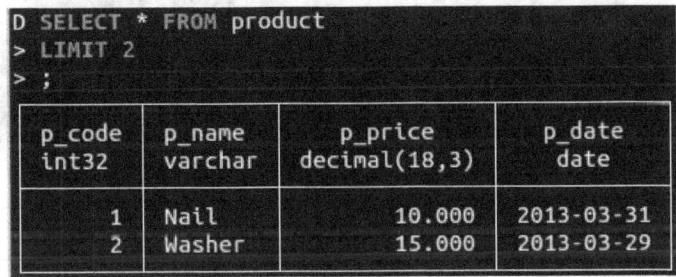

If you don't want the returned rows to start from the first row in the table, use OFFSET.

Example 2.17: Offset by 2

```
SELECT * FROM product
LIMIT 2 OFFSET 2
;
```

Instead of the first two rows, the returned rows are the third and fourth rows of the product table.

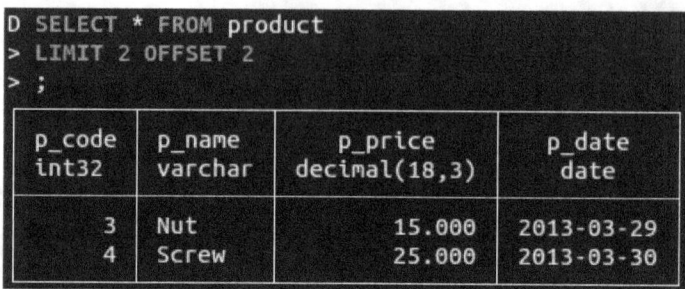

ORDER BY

If you want to order the returned rows, use ORDER BY.

Example 2.18 orders the returned rows by the product names in ascending order. If you omit ASC, it will still be ascending, as ASC is the default direction.

Example 2.18: Ascending ordering by product names

```
SELECT * FROM product
ORDER BY p_name ASC
;
```

The returned rows are correctly in ascending order on the product names.

```
D SELECT * FROM product
> ORDER BY p_name ASC
> ;
```

p_code int32	p_name varchar	p_price decimal(18,3)	p_date date
1	Nail	10.000	2013-03-31
6	New Nut		
3	Nut	15.000	2013-03-29
4	Screw	25.000	2013-03-30
5	Super_Nut	30.000	2013-03-30
2	Washer	15.000	2013-03-29

If you want your returned rows show up in descending order use DESC.

Example 2.19: Descending order

```
SELECT * FROM product
ORDER BY p_name DESC
;
```

The order of the returned is as expected.

```
D SELECT * FROM product
> ORDER BY p_name DESC
> ;

 p_code   p_name        p_price      p_date
 int32    varchar    decimal(18,3)    date

      2   Washer           15.000   2013-03-29
      5   Super_Nut        30.000   2013-03-30
      4   Screw            25.000   2013-03-30
      3   Nut              15.000   2013-03-29
      6   New Nut
      1   Nail             10.000   2013-03-31
```

Chapter 3: Functions

A function can have one or more parameter, or no parameter. A function has a syntax: FUNCTION_NAME(parameter1, parameter2, ...)

For example the absolute function has a syntax: ABS(numeric). When you use it, you should provide a value to be passed to the parameter. (Using a function is also known as *calling* a function or *invoking* a function) The value must be that of the data type, which in the case of ABS is numeric. (Note that the value you pass to a function's *parameter* is called *argument*)

DuckDB comes with various functions (built-in functions). In this chapter you will learn some, those that I used most frequently in my works with SQL.

Numeric functions

ABS(numeric)

ABS returns the absolute value of the numeric argument.

Our product table currently has the following rows:

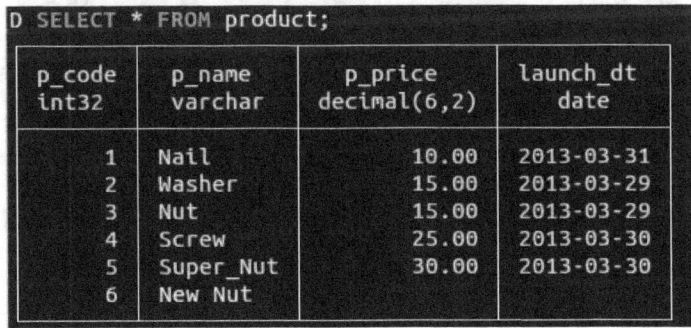

Let's add a row with a negative price:

```
INSERT INTO product VALUES(7, 'Hammer', -99, '2013-04-01');
```

```
D INSERT INTO product VALUES(7, 'Hammer', -99, '2013-04-01');
D SELECT * FROM product;
┌──────────┬───────────┬───────────────┬────────────┐
│ p_code   │ p_name    │ p_price       │ launch_dt  │
│ int32    │ varchar   │ decimal(6,2)  │ date       │
├──────────┼───────────┼───────────────┼────────────┤
│        1 │ Nail      │         10.00 │ 2013-03-31 │
│        2 │ Washer    │         15.00 │ 2013-03-29 │
│        3 │ Nut       │         15.00 │ 2013-03-29 │
│        4 │ Screw     │         25.00 │ 2013-03-30 │
│        5 │ Super_Nut │         30.00 │ 2013-03-30 │
│        6 │ New Nut   │               │            │
│        7 │ Hammer    │        -99.00 │ 2013-04-01 │
└──────────┴───────────┴───────────────┴────────────┘
```

And now we can try the ABS function:

```
SELECT p_name, ABS(p_price) FROM product;
```

```
D SELECT p_name, ABS(p_price) FROM product;
┌───────────┬───────────────┐
│ p_name    │ abs(p_price)  │
│ varchar   │ decimal(6,2)  │
├───────────┼───────────────┤
│ Nail      │         10.00 │
│ Washer    │         15.00 │
│ Nut       │         15.00 │
│ Screw     │         25.00 │
│ Super_Nut │         30.00 │
│ New Nut   │               │
│ Hammer    │         99.00 │
└───────────┴───────────────┘
```

SQRT(numeric)

SQRT returns the square root value of the numeric argument.

```
SELECT p_name, SQRT(p_price) FROM product WHERE p_price > 0;
```

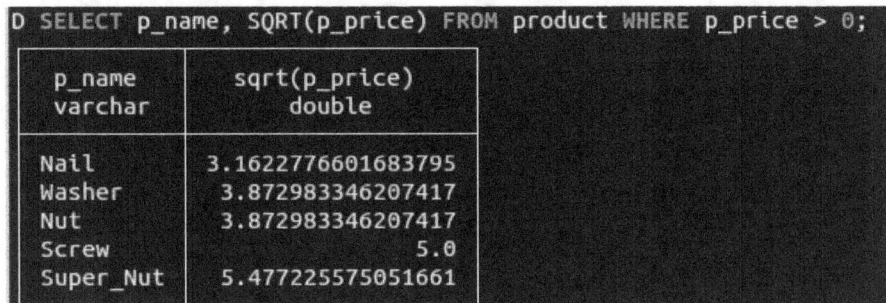

Note that in the query we filter out the negative price as the SQRT function does not handle negative argument. If you try a negative argument it will fail and you get an error message.

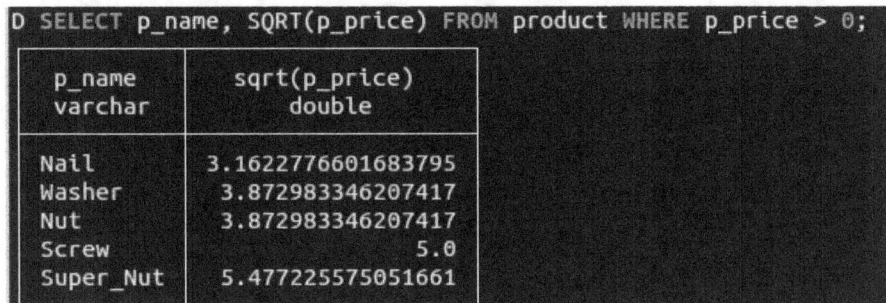

CEIL(numeric)

CEIL rounds up the numeric argument into an integer.

Let's insert two rows as follows:

```
INSERT INTO product
VALUES(8, 'New Hammer', 99.1, '2013-04-01'),
(9, 'New Washer', 10.01, '2013-05-01');
```

```
D INSERT INTO product
> VALUES(8, 'New Hammer', 99.1, '2013-04-01'),
> (9, 'New Washer', 10.01, '2013-05-01');
D SELECT * FROM product;
```

p_code int32	p_name varchar	p_price decimal(6,2)	launch_dt date
1	Nail	10.00	2013-03-31
2	Washer	15.00	2013-03-29
3	Nut	15.00	2013-03-29
4	Screw	25.00	2013-03-30
5	Super_Nut	30.00	2013-03-30
6	New Nut		
7	Hammer	-99.00	2013-04-01
8	New Hammer	99.10	2013-04-01
9	New Washer	10.01	2013-05-01

As you see below 99.1 is rounded to 100 and 10.00000010 is rounded to 11.

```
D SELeCT p_name, p_price, CEIL(p_price) FROM product;
```

p_name varchar	p_price decimal(6,2)	ceil(p_price) decimal(6,0)
Nail	10.00	10
Washer	15.00	15
Nut	15.00	15
Screw	25.00	25
Super_Nut	30.00	30
New Nut		
Hammer	-99.00	-99
New Hammer	99.10	100
New Washer	10.01	11

FLOOR(numeric)

FLOOR is the opposite of CEIL; it rounds down the numeric argument to an integer.

```
D SELeCT p_name, p_price, FLOOR(p_price) FROM product;
```

p_name varchar	p_price decimal(6,2)	floor(p_price) decimal(6,0)
Nail	10.00	10
Washer	15.00	15
Nut	15.00	15
Screw	25.00	25
Super_Nut	30.00	30
New Nut		
Hammer	-99.00	-99
New Hammer	99.10	99
New Washer	10.01	10

TEXT Functions

CONCAT(string1, string2, …)

CONCAT concatenates the string arguments.

I the following example CONCAT concatenates three strings: p_code, a dash, and p_name.

```
D SELECT CONCAT(p_code, ' - ', p_name), p_price FROM product;
 concat(p_code, ' - ', p_name)       p_price
            varchar               decimal(6,2)

 1 - Nail                               10.00
 2 - Washer                             15.00
 3 - Nut                                15.00
 4 - Screw                              25.00
 5 - Super_Nut                          30.00
 6 - New Nut
 7 - Hammer                            -99.00
 8 - New Hammer                         99.10
 9 - New Washer                         10.01
```

42

LENGTH(string, characters)

LENGTH counts the number of character in the string. Spaces are counted.

```
D SELECT p_name, LENGTH(p_name) FROM product;
```

p_name varchar	length(p_name) int64
Nail	4
Washer	6
Nut	3
Screw	5
Super_Nut	9
New Nut	7
Hammer	6
New Hammer	10
New Washer	10

LOWER(string) and UPPER(string)

LOWER and UPPER convert string to lowercase and uppercase, respectively.

```
D SELECT p_name, LOWER(p_name), UPPER(p_name) FROM product;
```

p_name varchar	lower(p_name) varchar	upper(p_name) varchar
Nail	nail	NAIL
Washer	washer	WASHER
Nut	nut	NUT
Screw	screw	SCREW
Super_Nut	super_nut	SUPER_NUT
New Nut	new nut	NEW NUT
Hammer	hammer	HAMMER
New Hammer	new hammer	NEW HAMMER
New Washer	new washer	NEW WASHER

SUBSTRING(string, start, length)

SUBSTRING extracts a sub-string from *string* of *length* characters starting from character *start*.

The following SUBSTRING extracts p_name starting from the first character for a length of four.

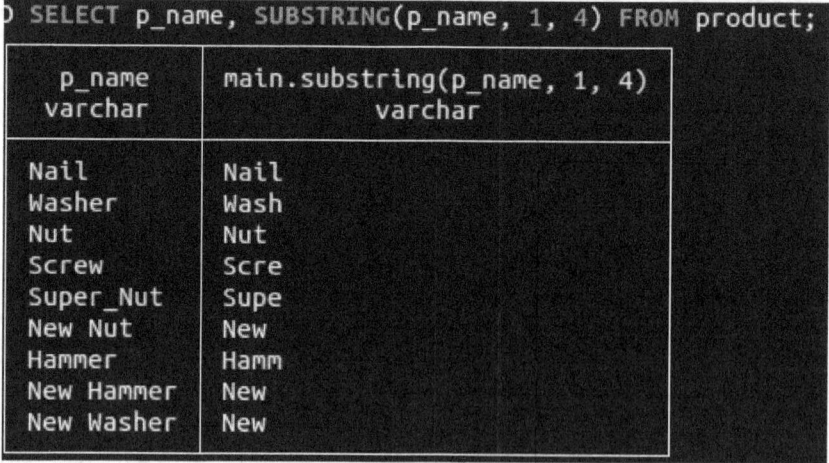

REPLACE(string, source, target)

REPLACE will replace *source* in the *string* with *target*.

In the following query string is p_name, source is New to be replace with NULL.

```
D SELECT p_name, REPLACE(p_name, 'New', 'Better') FROM product;
```

p_name varchar	replace(p_name, 'New', 'Better') varchar
Nail	Nail
Washer	Washer
Nut	Nut
Screw	Screw
Super_Nut	Super_Nut
New Nut	Better Nut
Hammer	Hammer
New Hammer	Better Hammer
New Washer	Better Washer

DATE Functions

CURRENT_DATE

CURRENT_DATE is the date when the SQL is executed.

```
D SELECT p_name, launch_dt, CURRENT_DATE FROM product;
```

p_name varchar	launch_dt date	current_date() date
Nail	2013-03-31	2023-05-14
Washer	2013-03-29	2023-05-14
Nut	2013-03-29	2023-05-14
Screw	2013-03-30	2023-05-14
Super_Nut	2013-03-30	2023-05-14
New Nut		2023-05-14
Hammer	2013-04-01	2023-05-14
New Hammer	2013-04-01	2023-05-14
New Washer	2013-05-01	2023-05-14

DATE_DIFF(*part*, **startdate**, *enddate*)

DATE_DIFF returns the difference between enddate and startdate. part can for examples be: year, month, day, and week.

```
D SELECT p_name, launch_dt,  DATE_DIFF('week', launch_dt, CURRENT_DATE) diff FROM product;

┌─────────────┬────────────┬───────┐
│   p_name    │ launch_dt  │ diff  │
│   varchar   │    date    │ int64 │
├─────────────┼────────────┼───────┤
│ Nail        │ 2013-03-31 │  528  │
│ Washer      │ 2013-03-29 │  528  │
│ Nut         │ 2013-03-29 │  528  │
│ Screw       │ 2013-03-30 │  528  │
│ Super_Nut   │ 2013-03-30 │  528  │
│ New Nut     │            │       │
│ Hammer      │ 2013-04-01 │  527  │
│ New Hammer  │ 2013-04-01 │  527  │
│ New Washer  │ 2013-05-01 │  523  │
└─────────────┴────────────┴───────┘
```

DATE_PART(part, date)

DATE_PART returns the *part* of a *date*. Part can for examples be: year, month, day, and week.

```
D SELECT p_name, launch_dt,
> DATE_PART('YEAR', launch_dt) yr,
> DATE_PART('WEEK', launch_dt) wk,
> DATE_PART('DAY', launch_dt) dy
> FROM product;
```

p_name varchar	launch_dt date	yr int64	wk int64	dy int64
Nail	2013-03-31	2013	13	31
Washer	2013-03-29	2013	13	29
Nut	2013-03-29	2013	13	29
Screw	2013-03-30	2013	13	30
Super_Nut	2013-03-30	2013	13	30
New Nut				
Hammer	2013-04-01	2013	14	1
New Hammer	2013-04-01	2013	14	1
New Washer	2013-05-01	2013	18	1

Chapter 4: Analytic Functions

In this chapter you will learn the various analytical functions provided by DuckDB. Let's start with some of the numerical functions.

Aggregate functions

While all previous queries operate on on individual row, the aggregate functions in Example 4.1 below work on all rows. The SUM(price) for example sums up the prices of all rows. Note that while count(price) does not include NULL in the counting, COUNT(*) does.

Example 4.1: Aggregates

```
SELECT SUM(p_price) s, AVG(p_price) a,
MAX(p_price) ma, MIN(p_price) mi,
COUNT(p_price) c, COUNT(*) cc
FROM product
;
```

As we aggregate all rows, we correctly get one returned row with the six aggregated columns.

```
D SELECT SUM(p_price) s, AVG(p_price) a,
> MAX(p_price) ma, MIN(p_price) mi,
> COUNT(p_price) c, COUNT(*) cc
> FROM product
> ;
```

s decimal(38,2)	a double	ma decimal(6,2)	mi decimal(6,2)	c int64	cc int64
105.11	13.13875	99.10	-99.00	8	9

Grouping

Example 4.1 aggregates the price of all rows together. If you need to aggregate by group for example launch date, use a GROUP BY, as in Example 4.2.

As we have three different launch dates and one NULL, the queries returned three rows.

Example 4.2: Aggregates by launch date

```
SELECT launch_dt,
SUM(p_price) s, AVG(p_price) a,
MAX(p_price) ma, MIN(p_price) mi,
COUNT(p_price) c, COUNT(*) cc
FROM product
GROUP BY launch_dt
;
```

The console shows the three "launch dates grouped" returned rows.

```
D SELECT launch_dt,
> SUM(p_price) s, AVG(p_price) a,
> MAX(p_price) ma, MIN(p_price) mi,
> COUNT(p_price) c, COUNT(*) cc
> FROM product
> GROUP BY launch_dt
> ;
```

launch_dt date	s decimal(38,2)	a double	ma decimal(6,2)	mi decimal(6,2)	c int64	cc int64
					0	1
2013-03-29	30.00	15.0	15.00	15.00	2	2
2013-03-30	55.00	27.5	30.00	25.00	2	2
2013-03-31	10.00	10.0	10.00	10.00	1	1
2013-04-01	0.10	0.05	99.10	-99.00	2	2
2013-05-01	10.01	10.01	10.01	10.01	1	1

Group condition (HAVING)

We use WHERE condition to select specific rows. If you need to select specific groups, use HAVING condition.

Here is the syntax.

```
SELECT columns, aggregate_function(group_columns)
FROM table(s)
WHERE condition
GROUP BY group_columns
HAVING group_condition
ORDER BY columns;
```

Example 4.3 has HAVING COUNT(price) > 1, hence only rows where the aggregated count are greater than 1 are returned by the query. Only Nut and Washer have the same price = 15, their aggregate count is then two and aggregate price is 30.

Example 4.3 HAVING clause

```
SELECT p_price, launch_dt,
SUM(p_price), COUNT(p_price)
FROM product
GROUP BY p_price, launch_dt
HAVING COUNT(p_price) > 1
;
```

Here is the returned row as expected.

```
D SELECT p_price, launch_dt,
> SUM(p_price), COUNT(p_price)
> FROM product
> GROUP BY p_price, launch_dt
> HAVING COUNT(p_price) > 1
> ;
```

p_price decimal(6,2)	launch_dt date	sum(p_price) decimal(38,2)	count(p_price) int64
15.00	2013-03-29	30.00	2

Cube

A cube is a row returned by a query that has a CUBE clause. Such a query return multiple cubes.

We'll use an inventory table for the cube examples, so please create and populate as follows.

```
CREATE TABLE inventory
(supplier VARCHAR(20)
, product VARCHAR(20)
, delivery_dt DATE
, quantity INTEGER)
;

INSERT INTO inventory
VALUES('North Nuts','Nut', '2013-03-31',1000),
('Toronto Tools','Washer', '2013-03-31',1500),
('Toronto Tools','Hammer', '2013-03-31',1500),
('North Nuts','Washer', '2013-04-01',1000),
('Toronto Tools','Nut', '2013-04-01',1500),
('North Nuts','Hammer', '2013-04-01',1000),
('North Nuts','Hammer', '2013-05-01',1000),
('North Nuts','Hammer', '2013-06-01',1000)
;
```

```
D CREATE TABLE inventory
> (supplier VARCHAR(20)
> , product VARCHAR(20)
> , delivery_dt DATE
> , quantity INTEGER)
> ;
D INSERT INTO inventory
> VALUES('North Nuts','Nut', '2013-03-31',1000),
> ('Toronto Tools','Washer', '2013-03-31',1500),
> ('Toronto Tools','Hammer', '2013-03-31',1500),
> ('North Nuts','Washer', '2013-04-01',1000),
> ('Toronto Tools','Nut', '2013-04-01',1500),
> ('North Nuts','Hammer', '2013-04-01',1000),
> ('North Nuts','Hammer', '2013-05-01',1000),
> ('North Nuts','Hammer', '2013-06-01',1000)
> ;
```

A cube has multiple dimensions. In Example 4.4, the cubes have three dimensions: supplier, product, and delivery_dt. These dimensions are the columns listed under the CUBE clause in the query. In other words, you specify the dimensions that you want by listing them under the CUBE clause.

The GROUP BY specifies the aggregation. In Example 4.4 the aggregation is sum and count.

Example 4.4 Cubes of inventory

```
SELECT supplier, product, delivery_dt,
SUM(quantity), count(quantity)
FROM inventory WHERE quantity is NOT NULL
GROUP BY CUBE (supplier,product,delivery_dt)
;
```

Here are all the inventory cubes returned by the CUBE query.

```
D SELECT supplier, product, delivery_dt,
> SUM(quantity), count(quantity)
> FROM inventory WHERE quantity is NOT NULL
> GROUP BY CUBE (supplier,product,delivery_dt)
> ;
```

supplier varchar	product varchar	delivery_dt date	sum(quantity) int128	count(quantity) int64
			9500	8
North Nuts			5000	5
Toronto Tools			4500	3
North Nuts	Nut		1000	1
Toronto Tools	Washer		1500	1
Toronto Tools	Hammer		1500	1
North Nuts	Washer		1000	1
Toronto Tools	Nut		1500	1
North Nuts	Hammer		3000	3
North Nuts	Nut	2013-03-31	1000	1
Toronto Tools	Washer	2013-03-31	1500	1
Toronto Tools	Hammer	2013-03-31	1500	1
North Nuts	Washer	2013-04-01	1000	1
Toronto Tools	Nut	2013-04-01	1500	1
North Nuts	Hammer	2013-04-01	1000	1
North Nuts	Hammer	2013-05-01	1000	1
North Nuts	Hammer	2013-06-01	1000	1
North Nuts		2013-03-31	1000	1
Toronto Tools		2013-03-31	3000	2
North Nuts		2013-04-01	2000	2
Toronto Tools		2013-04-01	1500	1
North Nuts		2013-05-01	1000	1
North Nuts		2013-06-01	1000	1
	Nut		2500	2
	Washer		2500	2
	Hammer		4500	4
	Nut	2013-03-31	1000	1
	Washer	2013-03-31	1500	1
	Hammer	2013-03-31	1500	1
	Washer	2013-04-01	1000	1
	Nut	2013-04-01	1500	1
	Hammer	2013-04-01	1000	1
	Hammer	2013-05-01	1000	1
	Hammer	2013-06-01	1000	1
		2013-03-31	4000	3
		2013-04-01	3500	3
		2013-05-01	1000	1
		2013-06-01	1000	1

| 38 rows | | | | 5 columns |

You can see that all possible combinations of the dimensions (values of the dimensions), including NULL, are in the returned rows. NULL means any value of that dimension.

Slice and dice

You can query a cube, selecting its rows by conditioning on the dimensions. In Example 4.5, we query the cube with the condition **WHERE supplier = 'North Nuts' AND product = 'Nut' AND delivery_dt IS NULL**.

Note that the cube query is within the query that has this condition. The cube query is called sub query. You will learn about sub query in Chapter 5.

Querying a cube as in Example 4.5 is popularly known as slice and dice. The query cut the cube into smaller cube.

Example 4.5: slice and dice

```
SELECT supplier, product, delivery_dt, cp, sp FROM
(SELECT supplier, product, delivery_dt,
count(quantity) cp, SUM(quantity) sp
FROM inventory
GROUP BY CUBE (supplier, product, delivery_dt))
WHERE supplier = 'North Nuts'
AND product = 'Nut'
AND delivery_dt IS NULL
;
```

Here's the resulting cube:

```
D SELECT supplier, product, delivery_dt, cp, sp FROM
> (SELECT supplier, product, delivery_dt,
> count(quantity) cp, SUM(quantity) sp
> FROM inventory
> GROUP BY CUBE (supplier, product, delivery_dt))
> WHERE supplier = 'North Nuts'
> AND product = 'Nut'
> AND delivery_dt IS NULL
> ;
```

supplier varchar	product varchar	delivery_dt date	cp int64	sp int128
North Nuts	Nut		1	1000

Window functions

The previous examples returned a row for each of the aggregated rows. The product table has **seven rows**, but when we run an aggregated query like the following one, the output is just **three aggregated rows.**

```
SELECT launch_dt, SUM(p_price)
FROM product
GROUP BY launch_dt
;
```

The three returned rows are:

```
D SELECT launch_dt, SUM(p_price)
> FROM product
> GROUP BY launch_dt
> ;

 launch_dt     sum(p_price)
   date        decimal(38,2)


 2013-03-29          30.00
 2013-03-30          55.00
 2013-03-31          10.00
 2013-04-01           0.10
 2013-05-01          10.01
```

When you need to have all rows prior to the grouping **and** each row has the aggregated column (sum column in our example query above), then use a window function. A window function is distinguished by the presence of an **OVER** clause in the query, such as in Example 4.6 below.

The PARTITION BY launch_dt inside the OVER clause in Example 4.6 grouped the rows by their launch date when computing the sum of their prices and put the result on the sum column of each rows (each of the seven rows)

Example 4.6: Window functionality

```
SELECT launch_dt, p_price, SUM(p_price)
OVER (PARTITION BY launch_dt)
FROM product
;
```

Here's the output of the window query. The sum(price) of the 2013-03-29 group from the two rows is (15 + 15) = 30; of the 2013-03-30 group is (25 + 30) = 55; and of the 203-03-31 group is just the one last row = 10.

```
D SELECT launch_dt, p_price, SUM(p_price)
> OVER (PARTITION BY launch_dt)
> FROM product
> ;

launch_dt      p_price      sum(p_price) OVER (PARTITION BY launch_dt)
date           decimal(6,2)              decimal(38,2)

2013-03-29       15.00                                          30.00
2013-03-29       15.00                                          30.00
2013-05-01       10.01                                          10.01
2013-04-01      -99.00                                           0.10
2013-04-01       99.10                                           0.10
2013-03-30       25.00                                          55.00
2013-03-30       30.00                                          55.00

2013-03-31       10.00                                          10.00
```

There is much more functionality of the window function than exemplified by the above example. You can learn more about window function in my other books: *Windowing for Analytic* and *Ranking and Such for Analytic* and *Learning Analytic in SQL for Beginners*. All of these books are also available from amazon bookstores.

Statistical functions

DuckDB, being designed with analytic capabilities in mind, has many other aggregate functions, including statistical functions.

Median and mode

Example 4.7 shows the use of median and mode functions.

Example 4.7: median and mode functions

```
SELECT median(price),
mode(price) FROM product
;
```

Here's the returned row:

```
D SELECT median(p_price),
> mode(p_price) FROM product
> ;
```

median(p_price) decimal(6,2)	mode(p_price) decimal(6,2)
15.00	15.00

Sample

SAMPLE randomly picks up the specified number of rows to be returned. Examples 4.8 uses SAMPLE. USING SAMPLE 2 requested the query to randomly return two rows. Note that the clause USING SAMPLE 2 resides after FROM product, not in the select list.

Example 4.8: Sample

```
SELECT * FROM product USING SAMPLE 2
;
```

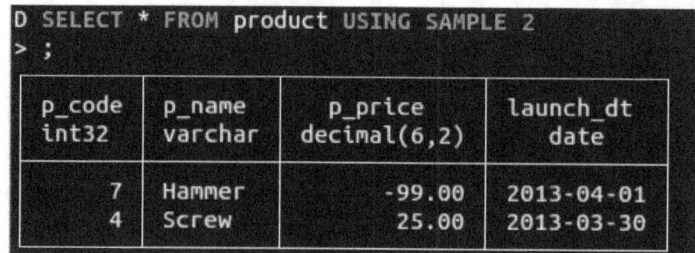

As the USING SAMPLE randomly picks up the number of rows (in our example two rows), the next time run the same query, the returned two rows can be different.

The following two returned rows were different when I ran that query again.

p_code int32	p_name varchar	p_price decimal(6,2)	launch_dt date
7	Hammer	-99.00	2013-04-01
4	Screw	25.00	2013-03-30

Chapter 5: Joins

A real-world database typically stores data in dozens or even hundreds of tables. In these multi-table databases, a table often relates to one or some other tables. In a query, you use JOIN to relate these tables. This chapter shows you how.

Here is the syntax of joins.

```
SELECT columns FROM table_1
JOIN table_2
ON table_1.column_1 = table_2.join_column_2
JOIN table_3
ON table_2.column_2 = table_3.join_column_3
JOIN …
```

For the join examples, you need to create two tables: customer and c_order (customer order)

Enter and execute the following two commands to create and populate customer table.

```
CREATE TABLE customer (c_no INT, c_name VARCHAR(20));

INSERT INTO customer
VALUES
(10, 'Standard Store'),
(20, 'Quality Store'),
(30, 'Head Office'),
(40, 'Super Agent')
;
```

```
D CREATE TABLE customer (c_no INT, c_name VARCHAR(20));
D INSERT INTO customer
> VALUES
> (10, 'Standard Store'),
> (20, 'Quality Store'),
> (30, 'Head Office'),
> (40, 'Super Agent')
> ;
D SELECT * FROM customer;

┌───────┬────────────────┐
│ c_no  │    c_name      │
│ int32 │    varchar     │
├───────┼────────────────┤
│    10 │ Standard Store │
│    20 │ Quality Store  │
│    30 │ Head Office    │
│    40 │ Super Agent    │
└───────┴────────────────┘
```

And then create and populate the other table, c_order, by entering and executing the following two commands:

```
CREATE TABLE c_order
(c_no INTEGER,
p_code INTEGER,
qty REAL,
order_dt DATE)
;

INSERT INTO c_order
VALUES (10, 1, 100, '2013-04-01')
, (10, 2, 100, '2013-04-01')
, (20, 1, 200, '2013-04-01')
, (30, 3, 300, '2013-04-02')
, (40, 4, 400, '2013-04-02')
, (40, 5, 400, '2013-04-03')
;
```

Here are the rows in the c_order table:

```
D SELECT * FROM c_order;
```

c_no int32	p_code int32	qty float	order_dt date
10	1	100.0	2013-04-01
10	2	100.0	2013-04-01
20	1	200.0	2013-04-01
30	3	300.0	2013-04-02
40	4	400.0	2013-04-02
40	5	400.0	2013-04-03

Two tables join

Example 5.1 is an example of a JOIN query. It joins the rows from the c_order table to the rows from the customer table based on their c_no columns. The query returns the name of every customer who has placed one or more orders.

Example 5.1: A two tables join

```
SELECT c_name, p_code,
c_order.qty, c_order.order_dt
FROM c_order JOIN customer
ON c_order.c_no = customer.c_no
;
```

The output is:

```
D SELECT c_name, p_code,
> c_order.qty, c_order.order_dt
> FROM c_order JOIN customer
> ON c_order.c_no = customer.c_no
> ;
```

c_name varchar	p_code int32	qty float	order_dt date
Standard Store	1	100.0	2013-04-01
Standard Store	2	100.0	2013-04-01
Quality Store	1	200.0	2013-04-01
Head Office	3	300.0	2013-04-02
Super Agent	4	400.0	2013-04-02
Super Agent	5	400.0	2013-04-03

Three tables join

From the JOIN syntax presented earlier, you can join more than two tables. To do this, in the SELECT statement, join two tables at a time.

Example 5.2 is a query with three tables join

Example 5.2: Product joins to customer and c_order

```
SELECT c_name, p_name, o.qty, o.order_dt
FROM c_order o
JOIN customer c ON o.c_no = c.c_no
JOIN product p ON o.p_code = p.p_code
;
```

The result is shown below.

```
D SELECT c_name, p_name, o.qty, o.order_dt
> FROM c_order o
> JOIN customer c ON o.c_no = c.c_no
> JOIN product p ON o.p_code = p.p_code
> ;
```

c_name varchar	p_name varchar	qty float	order_dt date
Quality Store	Nail	200.0	2013-04-01
Standard Store	Washer	100.0	2013-04-01
Head Office	Nut	300.0	2013-04-02
Super Agent	Screw	400.0	2013-04-02
Super Agent	Super_Nut	400.0	2013-04-03
Standard Store	Nail	100.0	2013-04-01

Joining on More than One Column

The preceding joins were on one column. Tables can also be joined on more than one column.

Before you try the next examples, please create the following shipment table and insert the rows using the following SQL statements.

```
CREATE TABLE shipment (
c_no INT,
p_code INT,
order_dt DATE,
ship_qty INT,
ship_dt DATE)
;

INSERT INTO shipment
VALUES (10, 1, '2013-04-01', 50, '2013-04-02')
, (10, 2, '2013-04-01', 100, '2013-04-02')
, (20, 1, '2013-04-01', 100, '2013-04-02')
, (30, 3, '2013-04-02', 300, '2013-04-03')
, (10, 1, '2013-04-01', 50, '2013-04-10')
;
```

To retrieve the order quantity (the qty column of the c_order table) of each shipment, you need to have a query that joins the shipment table to the order table on three columns, c_no, p_no, and order_dt, as shown in the query in Example 5.3. Note the use of USING, instead of ON. Using USING you just mention the columns used to join the tables. You can use USING only when the columns used to join have the same name on two tables.

Example 5.3: joining on three columns

```
SELECT o.c_no, o.p_code
, o.order_dt, ship_qty
, ship_dt, qty
FROM shipment s JOIN c_order o
USING(c_no, p_code, order_dt);
```

Here is the output:

```
D SELECT o.c_no, o.p_code
>  , o.order_dt, ship_qty
>  , ship_dt, qty
> FROM shipment s JOIN c_order o
> USING(c_no, p_code, order_dt);
```

c_no int32	p_code int32	order_dt date	ship_qty int32	ship_dt date	qty float
10	1	2013-04-01	50	2013-04-10	100.0
10	2	2013-04-01	100	2013-04-02	100.0
20	1	2013-04-01	100	2013-04-02	200.0
30	3	2013-04-02	300	2013-04-03	300.0
10	1	2013-04-01	50	2013-04-02	100.0

Left Outer Join

All the joins I explained so far were inner joins. A LEFT OUTER JOIN query produces all rows from the table on the left of the left outer join will be in the output whether or not there are matching rows from the table on its right. The syntax for the left outer join is as follows.

```
SELECT columns
FROM table_1 LEFT OUTER JOIN table_2
ON table_1.column = table_2.column ...
```

The query in Example 5.4 has a left outer join. This query returns all rows from the c_order table.

Example 5.4 left outer join

```
SELECT o.*, ship_dt
FROM c_order o
LEFT OUTER JOIN shipment s
ON o.p_code = s.p_code
AND o.c_no = s.c_no
;
```

The result of the query is as follows. Note that the two orders at the bottom by customer number 40 have not been shipped, as indicated by the blanks on the ship_dt.

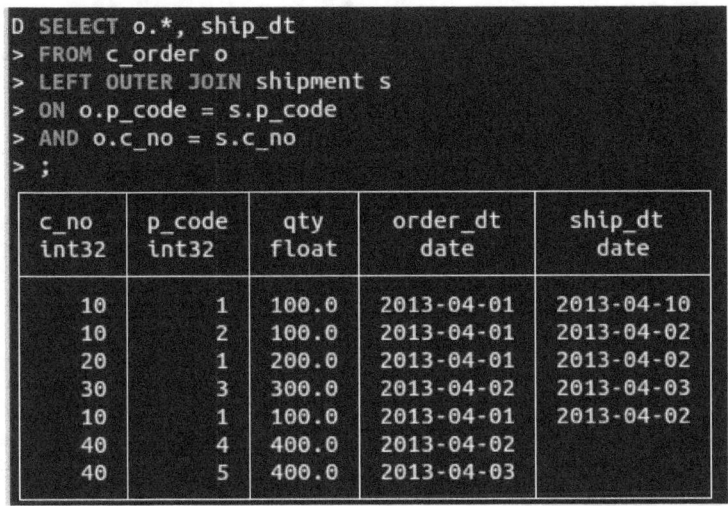

```
D SELECT o.*, ship_dt
> FROM c_order o
> LEFT OUTER JOIN shipment s
> ON o.p_code = s.p_code
> AND o.c_no = s.c_no
> ;
```

c_no int32	p_code int32	qty float	order_dt date	ship_dt date
10	1	100.0	2013-04-01	2013-04-10
10	2	100.0	2013-04-01	2013-04-02
20	1	200.0	2013-04-01	2013-04-02
30	3	300.0	2013-04-02	2013-04-03
10	1	100.0	2013-04-01	2013-04-02
40	4	400.0	2013-04-02	
40	5	400.0	2013-04-03	

Self-Joins

Assuming some of your products have substitutes and you want to record the substitutes in the product table, you then need to add a column. The new column, which is called s_code in the product table, contains the product code of the substitute.

To add the s_code column, execute the following statement:

```
ALTER TABLE product
ADD s_code integer
;
```

Then, to update the p_code = 3 row, execute the following statement:

```
UPDATE product
SET s_code = 5
WHERE p_code = 3
;
```

The product table now has the following rows. Notice the s_code value is 5 for p_code = 3.

```
SELECT * from product
;
```

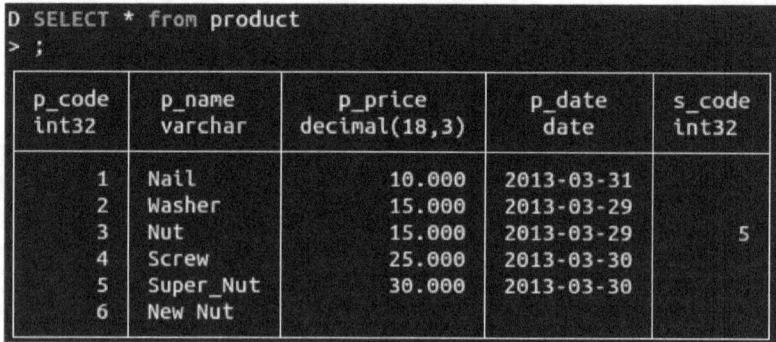

Note that s_code = 5 is Super_Nut.

If you need to know the product name of a substitute, you need the query shown in Example 5.5. This query joins the product table to itself. This kind of join is called a self-join.

The syntax for the self join is as follows.

```
SELECT columns
FROM table alias_1
JOIN table alias_2
ON alias_1.column_x = alias_2.column_y
```

Note that *column_x* and *column_y* are columns in the same table.

Example 5.5: A self-join

```
SELECT prod.p_code, prod.p_name,
subst.p_code subst_p_code,
subst.p_name subst_name
FROM product prod
LEFT OUTER JOIN product subst
ON prod.s_code = subst.p_code
ORDER BY prod.p_code
;
```

Here are the returned rows of the query, showing "Super_Nut on the subst_name column of the third row.

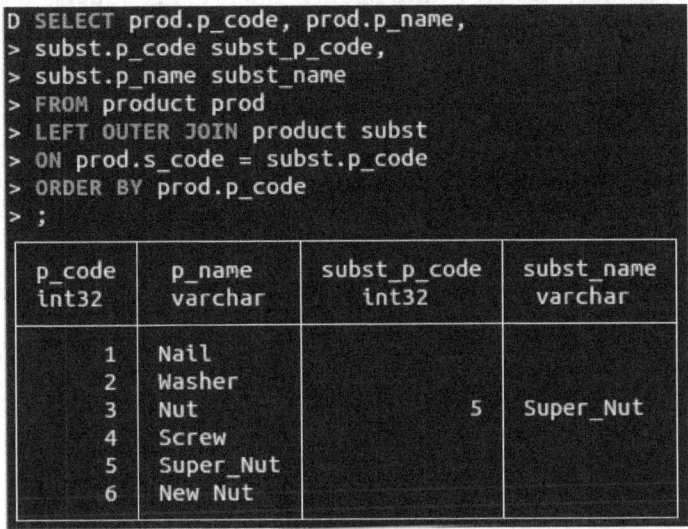

```
D SELECT prod.p_code, prod.p_name,
> subst.p_code subst_p_code,
> subst.p_name subst_name
> FROM product prod
> LEFT OUTER JOIN product subst
> ON prod.s_code = subst.p_code
> ORDER BY prod.p_code
> ;
```

p_code int32	p_name varchar	subst_p_code int32	subst_name varchar
1	Nail		
2	Washer		
3	Nut	5	Super_Nut
4	Screw		
5	Super_Nut		
6	New Nut		

Chapter 6: Sub queries

A subquery is a query nested within another query. A subquery in turn can have a nested query, making it a multiple nested query. The subquery is also known as inner query; the enclosing query, outer query.

The examples in this chapter uses the original product table, that is before we added the product substitute s_code column. So, you need to run the following commands:

```
DROP TABLE product;

CREATE TABLE product
(p_code INT, p_name VARCHAR(20)
, price DECIMAL(6,2), launch_dt DATE)
;

INSERT INTO product
VALUES (1, 'Nail', 10.0, '2013-03-31')
, (2, 'Washer', 15.00, '2013-03-29')
, (3, 'Nut', 15.00, '2013-03-29')
, (4, 'Screw', 25.00, '2013-03-30')
, (5, 'Super_Nut', 30.00, '2013-03-30')
, (6, 'New Nut', NULL, NULL)
;
```

```
D SELECT * FROM product;
```

p_code int32	p_name varchar	price decimal(6,2)	launch_dt date
1	Nail	10.00	2013-03-31
2	Washer	15.00	2013-03-29
3	Nut	15.00	2013-03-29
4	Screw	25.00	2013-03-30
5	Super_Nut	30.00	2013-03-30
6	New Nut		

Single value sub query

A single value subquery is a subquery that returns a single value. A single-row subquery can be placed in the WHERE clause of an outer query. The return value of the subquery is compared with a column of the outer query using one of the comparison operators.

The subquery (printed in bold) in Example 6.1 returns the highest price among the prices of products that have been ordered. The outer query returns all products from the product table that have that highest price (in the example, 30.00), which is Super_Nut.

Example 6.1: A sub query returning a single value

```
SELECT * FROM product
WHERE price =
(SELECT MAX(price) FROM product)
;
```

The query returns the Super_Nut as expected.

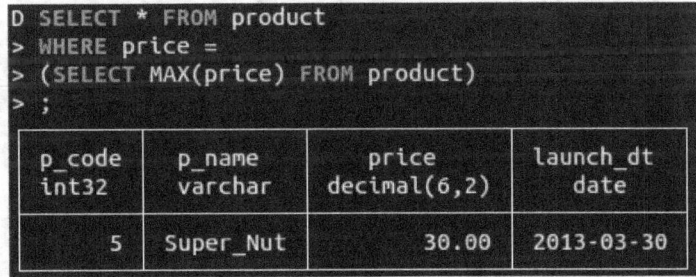

Note that the column and subquery result do not have to be the same column, but they must have compatible data types. In the query in Example 5.1, the price column of the product table is a numeric type and the subquery also returns a numeric type.

Multiple-values sub query

A subquery might return more than one row. If your outer query purposely intend to use all rows returning by the subquery, then use IN or NOT IN instead of = (equal to).

For example, the query in Example 6.2 contains a multiple-values subquery. The inner query returns all nut-like products (p_code's)

Example 6.2: IN subquery

```
SELECT * FROM product
WHERE p_code
IN (
SELECT p_code FROM product
WHERE p_name LIKE '%Nut%')
;
```

The query returns the three nut-like's as expected.

```
D SELECT * FROM product
> WHERE p_code
> IN (
> SELECT p_code FROM product
> WHERE p_name LIKE '%Nut%')
> ;
```

p_code int32	p_name varchar	price decimal(6,2)	launch_dt date
3	Nut	15.00	2013-03-29
5	Super_Nut	30.00	2013-03-30
6	New Nut		

Nested sub queries

A subquery can contain a subquery as in Example 6.3. The first inner query returns all three products having names contain Nut. But, the inner most query return only products that have a launch date. Hence, the whole query returns only Nut and Super_Nut.

Example 6.3: Nested sub queries

```
SELECT * FROM product WHERE p_code
IN (
SELECT p_code FROM product
WHERE p_name LIKE '%Nut%'
AND
price IN (
SELECT price FROM product
WHERE launch_dt IS NOT NULL))
;
```

The query returns the two rows as expected.

```
D SELECT * FROM product WHERE p_code
> IN (
> SELECT p_code FROM product
> WHERE p_name LIKE '%Nut%'
> AND
> price IN (
> SELECT price FROM product
> WHERE launch_dt IS NOT NULL))
> ;
```

p_code int32	p_name varchar	price decimal(6,2)	launch_dt date
3	Nut	15.00	2013-03-29
5	Super_Nut	30.00	2013-03-30

Correlated Sub queries

All the preceding sub queries are independent of their outer queries. A subquery can also be related to its outer query, where one or more column from the outer query table is (are) related to the column(s) of the subquery table in the WHERE clause of the subquery. This type of subquery is called the correlated subquery.

Example 6.4 has a correlated subquery as it has the product codes from itself and its outer query related.

Example 6.4: Correlated subqueries

```
SELECT * FROM product oq WHERE price
IN
(SELECT iq.price FROM product iq
WHERE iq.p_name LIKE 'N%'
AND iq.p_code = oq.p_code)
;
```

The query returns the products that have the name starting with N.

```
D SELECT * FROM product oq WHERE price
> IN
> (SELECT iq.price FROM product iq
> WHERE iq.p_name LIKE 'N%'
> AND iq.p_code = oq.p_code)
> ;
```

p_code int32	p_name varchar	price decimal(6,2)	launch_dt date
1	Nail	10.00	2013-03-31
3	Nut	15.00	2013-03-29
6	New Nut		

Chapter 7: CTE (Common Table Expression)

For better readability you can put subqueries in the WITH clause. A query in the WITH clause is known as Common Table Expression or CTE for short.

Sub queries as CTE

The two sub queries in Example 6.3 is written as two CTE's in Example 7.1 below. The two CTE's are named pc and pr respectively. They are then used in the query.

Example 7.1: CTE

```
WITH
pc AS (SELECT p_code FROM product WHERE p_name LIKE '%Nut%'),
pr AS (SELECT price FROM product WHERE launch_dt IS NOT NULL)
SELECT * FROM product p
WHERE p_code IN (select * from pc)
;
```

The returned rows are the same as that of Example 5.3.

```
D WITH
> pc AS (SELECT p_code FROM product WHERE p_name LIKE '%Nut%'),
> pr AS (SELECT price FROM product WHERE launch_dt IS NOT NULL)
> SELECT * FROM product p
> WHERE p_code IN (select * from pc)
> ;
```

p_code int32	p_name varchar	price decimal(6,2)	launch_dt date
3	Nut	15.00	2013-03-29
5	Super_Nut	30.00	2013-03-30
6	New Nut		

Nested CTE

You can nest CTE as demonstrated in Example 7.2 below. You might have noticed that nesting CTE is like developing incrementally. The first CTE selects Nut like product; then, the second, filtering out the selected products returned by the first CTE that do not have launch date. Of course, you can do joins instead of CTE, but imagine if you have many joins, the CTE version is likely easier to read and understand.

Example 7.2: Nested CTE

```
WITH
pc AS (SELECT * FROM product WHERE p_name LIKE '%Nut%'),
pr AS (SELECT * FROM pc WHERE launch_dt IS NOT NULL)
SELECT * FROM pr
;
```

The result will just be the same as expected.

```
D WITH
> pc AS (SELECT * FROM product WHERE p_name LIKE '%Nut%'),
> pr AS (SELECT * FROM pc WHERE launch_dt IS NOT NULL)
> SELECT * FROM pr
> ;
```

p_code int32	p_name varchar	price decimal(6,2)	launch_dt date
3	Nut	15.00	2013-03-29
5	Super_Nut	30.00	2013-03-30

Chapter 8: Views

A view is a predefined query. When a view is used the query is run. When the data against which the query is run, gets updated, the view gives you the updated data. You create a view using a CREATE VIEW statement.

Here is the syntax of the CREATE VIEW statement.

CREATE VIEW view_name (view_columns) AS (query)

A compelling reason to use view is to expose only selected columns and/or rows, any other data are sensitive and can be seen or used for secured purpose only. Access can only be by way of view, direct access to the table is not permitted.

You can turn all queries in the preceding chapters into views. Example 8.1 turns the query from Example 2.6 into a view. Note that the query's condition filters out product with price 25 or higher.

You query a view using the SELECT statement as you query a table.

The first command creates v_product view; the second command uses the view.

Example 8.1 View to secure product data

```
CREATE VIEW v_product AS
(SELECT p_name, price FROM product
WHERE price < 25)
;

SELECT * FROM v_product;
```

```
D CREATE VIEW v_product AS
> (SELECT p_name, price FROM product
> WHERE price < 25)
> ;
D SELECT * FROM v_product;

 p_name      price
 varchar     decimal(6,2)

 Nail            10.00
 Washer          15.00
 Nut             15.00
```

Nested Views

The query of a view can be on a view, hence creating a nested view. Example 8.2 is an example of a nested view. The v_nest_product is view created over the v_product we created in Example 8.1.

```
CREATE VIEW v_nest_product AS
(SELECT * FROM v_product
WHERE p_name <> 'Nail')
;
```

```
D CREATE VIEW v_nest_product AS
> (SELECT * FROM v_product
> WHERE p_name <> 'Nail')
> ;
D
D SELECT * FROM v_nest_product;
```

p_name varchar	price decimal(6,2)
Washer	15.00
Nut	15.00

Appendix: DuckDB CLI (Command Line Interface)

Follow this appendix helps your preparation to try the book examples.

Downloading

Download CLI from https://duckdb.org/docs/installation/index
Select the installation zip file for your platform. In my case I selected the first one, Linux 64-bit.

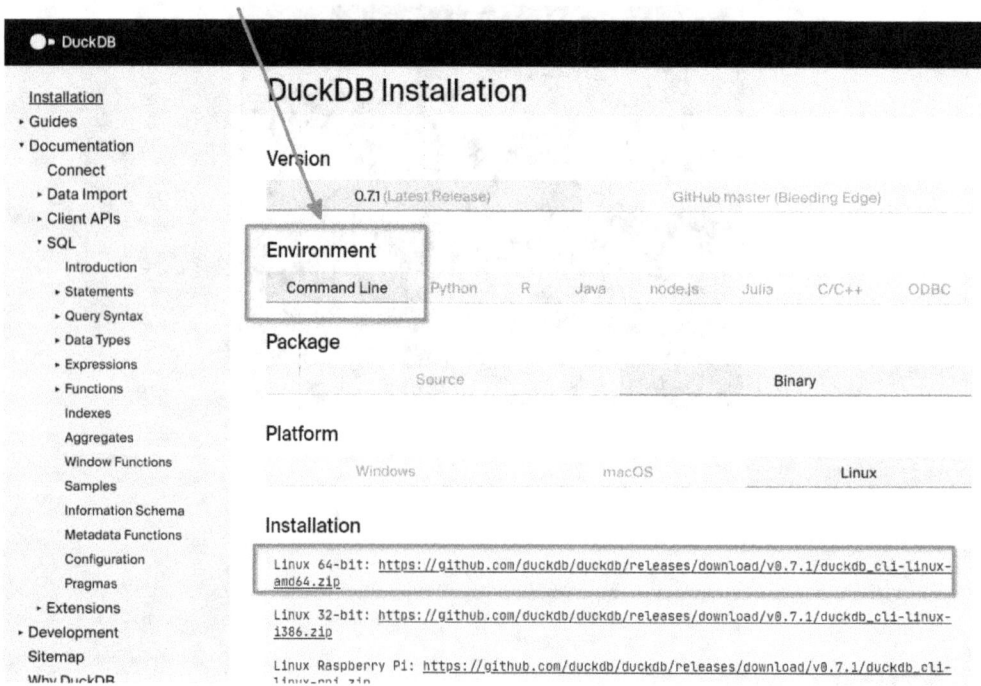

Installing

Extract the downloaded zip file into a folder of your choice. When extraction is completed, under that folder you should have a sub folder where you have a file duck**db.**

That's all you need. You use this file to run CLI , and then create a database and all its object. There**'s nothing else, like database server to install and maintain.**

In my case, I extracted to CLI. So, in my Ubuntu terminal, I can see the duckdb like the following:

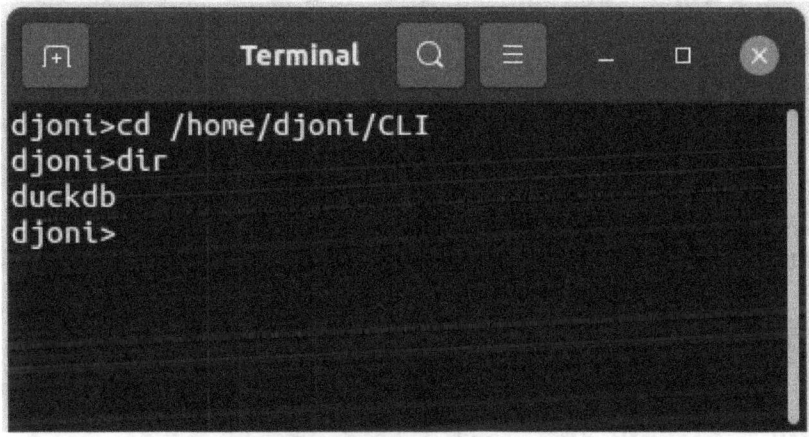

Using

To start the duckdb CLI terminal, run the duckdb file as follows:

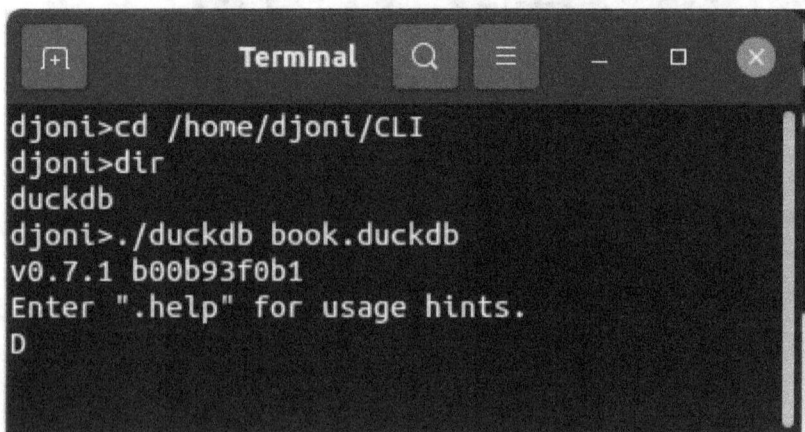

```
djoni>cd /home/djoni/CLI
djoni>./duckdb
v0.7.1 b00b93f0b1
Enter ".help" for usage hints.
Connected to a transient in-memory database.
Use ".open FILENAME" to reopen on a persistent database.
D
```

To create a new database, for example a database named book.duckdb, run the following. If the database already exists, it will be opened.

```
djoni>cd /home/djoni/CLI
djoni>dir
duckdb
djoni>./duckdb book.duckdb
v0.7.1 b00b93f0b1
Enter ".help" for usage hints.
D
```

To exit DuckDB CLI, press ctrl + d. You will be back to your Unix terminal.

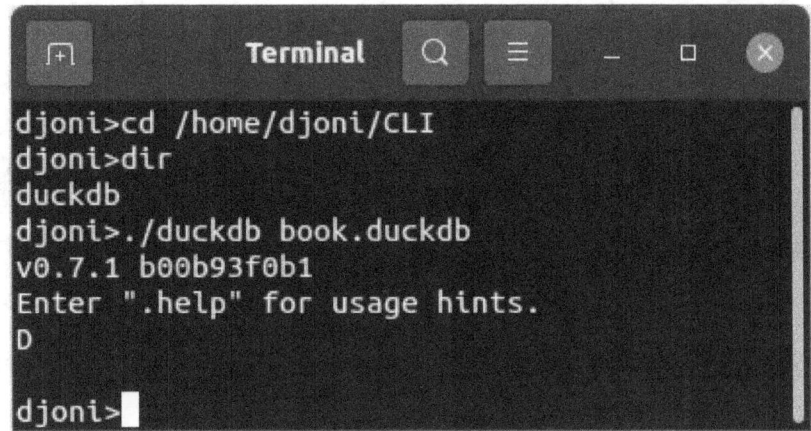

Now that you are on the DuckDB CLI, you can run SQL statement.

To start with, create a schema. Below I created a schema named book_**schema in t**he book **dat**abase. Don't forget to terminate your SQL with a semicolon.

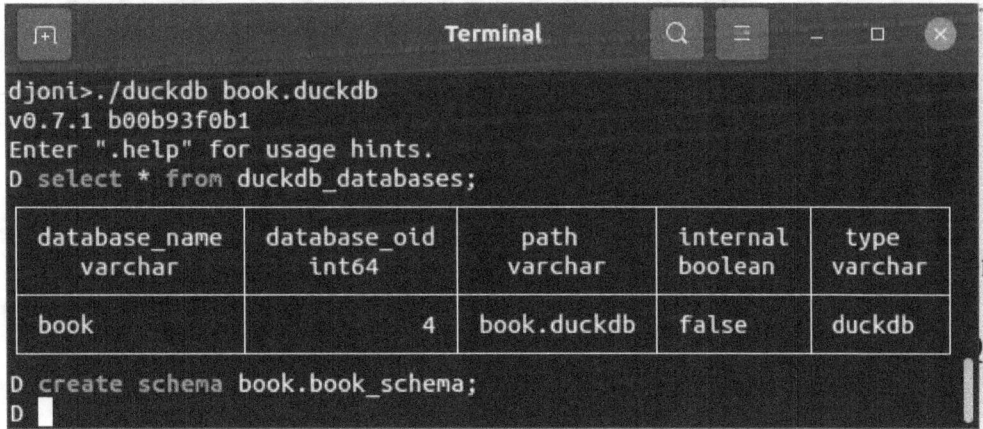

You can display the schema by running a select * from duckdb_schemas statement as follows:

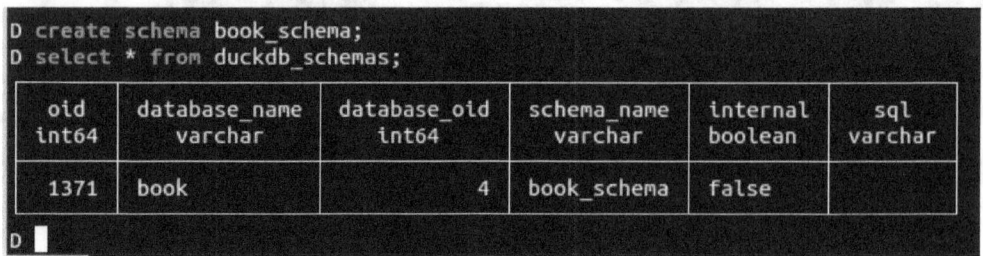

```
D create schema book_schema;
D select * from duckdb_schemas;
```

oid int64	database_name varchar	database_oid int64	schema_name varchar	internal boolean	sql varchar
1371	book	4	book_schema	false	

```
D
```

Next, let's create table named dummy with just one column, of type integer. To confirm the table was created, you can query the duck_tables built in data dictionary's table duckdb_tables.

```
D create table dummy (d integer);
D select schema_name, table_name from duckdb_tables;
```

schema_name varchar	table_name varchar
main	dummy

The dummy table we just created is under the **main s**chema. We actually wanted the table under our own schema, book_schema. We can do so by using a dot notation schemaname.tablename as follows.

```
D create table book_schema.dummy (d integer);
D select schema_name, table_name from duckdb_tables;
```

schema_name varchar	table_name varchar
book_schema main	dummy dummy

```
D
```

If you will often work with the book_schema, rather than prefixing with the schema-name, you can set book_schema as a **default** schema. Then when you create a table that you want it under the default schema, you don't need to specify the schema.

Below we set book_schema as the default schema. Then, we create dummy2 table with out specifying any schema. The dummy2 is created under book_schema.

```
D set schema to book_schema;
D create table dummy2(d1 text);
D select schema_name, table_name from duckdb_tables;
```

schema_name varchar	table_name varchar
book_schema book_schema main	dummy2 dummy dummy

www.ingramcontent.com/pod-product-compliance
Lightning Source LLC
Chambersburg PA
CBHW080612220526
45466CB00010B/3320